the prescription for JOY

How to transform yourself from overwhelmed to overjoyed

by Ruth R. Williams, LCSW

The Prescription for Joy: How to Transform Yourself from
Overwhelmed to Overjoyed

ISBN 978-1-45381-512-0

I would like to dedicate this literary adventure to my parents,
who ended up being my teachers in so many ways . . .
much to my surprise (and possibly theirs!).

But mostly, I wish to dedicate this to my sweet daughter,
whose love and affection have filled me with joy
I had barely imagined possible.

My Ecstasy

Ecstasy is . . .
Making, baking, smelling, tasting and sharing bread.
A cool breeze on a hot day or the sun's warm touch on a cool day.
The delicate aroma of honeysuckle tickling your nostrils.
Skies in all combinations—day and night, star-filled,
cloud-decorated, full moon, no moon—even rain and storm clouds
(skies are my very favorite of favorites!).
I especially like sunsets.
And rainbows are an extraordinary gift when they appear.
Water—big or small—flowing or still—in it, on it, by it, even
drinking it or showering or bathing in it,
It's cleansing, renewing, refreshing, calming—water.
Kitty cats and puppy dogs—stroking them, playing fetch or keepaway,
listening to them purr or bark, cuddling,
unconditionally loving.
Children . . . playful and mischievous, kind and innocent . . .
signs of hope and of timelessness.
A gift and an opportunity to give of yourself.
Having a cup of tea with honey in one of grandma's special tea cups,
listening to stories and learning about life.
Cheesecake . . . mmmmmm.
Creating a song, a picture, a photograph, a story.
Singing—at the top of my lungs or in a whisper, by myself
or with a partner or an entire choir.
Dreaming—daytime or nighttime.
Blossoms awakening on a long-quiet velvet violet.
A good cry at a great movie.
Getting lost in a kaleidoscope world.
Giggling and laughing out loud
while playing a board game with special friends.
Choosing to celebrate a tradition with your family—
getting all tingly inside.

Falling asleep on a comfy pillow in a cozy bed.
Standing quietly in the shelter of a young tree's leafy branches
Or hugging one of the older knotty majestic trees.
Swishing through rustling fallen leaves
or slushing through freshly fallen snow . . .
Anticipating buds bursting forth in the spring.
Dancing wildly to loud rock and roll or really close
with someone you love, to a sweet love song.
Praying and meditating . . .
Merging . . .
into the awesome unity and synchronicity of the universe.
Ecstasy for me is an everyday occurrence.
I am grateful.

—Ruth Ransdell Williams
12-1-2000

*This was composed prior to leading a workshop
for the local Alcohol & Drug Council,
offering some of Ruth's alternatives
to the street drug "Ecstasy."*

Table of Contents

Introduction

The Prescription
for Joy

Introduction

"You will never be happy if you continue to search for what happiness consists of. You will never live if you are looking for the meaning of life."
—*Albert Camus*

I'm hoping some of you opening the pages of this book are indeed happy and full of joy. I'm also hoping many of you are at ease with life instead of being filled with dis-ease (i.e., "out of ease"). Based on the growing number of folks who are physically ill or emotionally distraught (clearly evidenced by outrageously large numbers of prescriptions being filled on a daily basis), my guess is that you may be one of the over-stressed and overwhelmed. Trust me, more people are stressed than not.

So, is it the world we're living in that's the problem? It definitely contributes to dis-ease. All it takes is clicking the "on" button on the remote control—and voila, STRESS! It doesn't even have to be a news channel. Or leave the TV off, and just wait for your alarm to ring. The day begins. Stress begins. We all live there.

The number of people diagnosed with depression has skyrocketed in the last couple of decades. What's up?

Are we all biochemically malfunctioning? Is there something in the water? Maybe it's all the bottled water we've been drinking. Or the caffeine. Or food additives. Or pollution. Or global warming. Most of us had rotten childhoods—that's it! Let's blame it on dysfunctional families. Or, even better, let's blame it on the media. Or on politicians. Or on the latest supermodel or professional athlete or rock star. There are all kinds of places we can point fingers, fussing about the current state of affairs. But blaming never helped anyone—at least not that I can tell. So, what else should we consider?

There are many factors contributing to our unhappiness and to the dis-ease in our bodies, minds, and spirits. I believe the biggest culprit is STRESS! The "S word." Yes, folks, stress gets to us all. Research does show that a little bit of stress may work to your advantage. A moderate sense of urgency before an exam or a big project may help you be more prepared, more alert and "wired" in a positive way. However, when you turn that into more chronic, long-term stress, look out!

Another significant factor is that our families are often a mess. And one affects the other: Stress affects how our families function, and how our families function affects our personal stress level.

The dysfunction (family funk) is often passed on from generation to generation. One seemingly inevitable consequence, I believe, is that we're becoming bigger consumers, trying to "buy" our way to happiness, going for external versus internal contentment. So we're breeding a generation of computer/electronic device/TV/video game "junkies" and overeating, over-consuming, unhappy, drug-popping kids and adults. That doesn't sound happy, peaceful, or satisfied—any of the "ah" and "oh" words I personally seek out on an everyday basis—now, does it?

So our families are a mess, our emotions are a mess, and life is stressful! And our health is a mess as a result. I'm no doctor; however, I do know that more and more research is pointing to stress as a factor in all kinds of physical health issues (including cancer, heart disease, and even obesity). It's time to get it together, people! Time's a-wastin'. We cannot afford to let our immune systems crash because we're not managing our lives in healthy ways.

I do believe people are looking for answers and for a sense of meaning and purpose in their lives. We all want our lives to make sense, but sadly, it's not working very well. As a whole, many of us are just not happy. In fact, many of us are even clinically depressed—and antidepressants are now among the most frequently prescribed medications. Some recent estimates run as high as $10 billion a year in sales.

There's a lot of discussion—even controversy—regarding whether or not people who are receiving antidepressants are all indeed clinically depressed. Some also contend that medication in some cases may even mask problems that really need to be addressed.

I sometimes recommend consultation with a physician for folks who come to me for psychotherapy. Some clients come to me at the recommendation of a physician who is already prescribing antidepressants for them. For many individuals, antidepressant therapy has literally been a life-saver.

Some may see this increased use of antidepressants as a cause for celebration—i.e., as an indication that depression, anxiety, and other illnesses are finally being recognized and treated. Others may believe they are being over-prescribed. Whatever your opinion, you'll probably agree that prevention is key in our journey to health and wholeness. You may also agree that we need to look a little deeper to see if there are any changes we can make to help reduce the overall dis-ease we are experiencing.

We are a mess! (Well, maybe we aren't *all* a mess . . .)
And we do need some additional help in combating all the
stress accumulating in our lives. I'd like to offer a solution
that doesn't come in a pill.

I believe what we need more of to help us with the
"S word" is the "J word." We need to relearn simple, easily-
accessible, available (every single day of our lives) ways to
be inspired, enlightened, energized. I believe JOY is the
secret potion, the secret notion, the key! Joy sounds like a
simple enough "ingredient" and/or prescription. Children
tend to "get it" more than adults do, because as grown-ups
we start losing the ability to experience everyday joy. (And
I'm sad to say we often end up pushing our children into
the pressure-filled adult world way too soon.)

I've been blessed to be a "joy-seeker" (and "joy-
keeper") since I was a little girl. I may not have had the
words to describe it yet at four years old, but I certainly
knew how to take advantage of it! I want to share what I
have gained from my own life experience and from that of
many others with whom I've worked through the years in
my professional life as a clinical social worker.

In speaking about one's ability to be a joy-seeker
and a joy-keeper, I occasionally use the term "JQ." Just as

we have been aware of "IQ"—the intelligence quotient—and, more recently, "EQ"—referring to emotional intelligence—I'm using "JQ" as the "Joy Quotient," representing the joy factor that lives in your spirit and soul, in the depths of who you are at your core. Your JQ symbolically represents just how "high" you are able to go at enJOYing life. We don't need a number (as with IQ) because it's much more about perception, intuition, knowingness, and connection to the divine and eternal—all difficult to quantify, but very real nonetheless.

My goal is to help you reawaken your own innate ability to experience joy in the most easily accessible ways—every single day of your life! As you follow me through the concepts and Joy Rx Tips presented in each chapter (the ingredients of the Joy Prescription which raise your JQ), you will discover, uncover, or recover your innate ability to deal with life and what it hands you. Trust me—stuff happens! I'm sure you've already had what you consider "your share," and it probably won't stop there. I believe we're all here on this delightful planet Earth to learn, to become better people, to serve others, and to help make it the very best place to live in the galaxy.

Life is stressful. That's its job. Honestly, I think

that's how we learn—by going through stressful things. It builds "muscle," so to speak. And since stress affects absolutely everything, when you find your "J-spot"—your own personal avenue to joy—and when you begin increasing your own unique joy quotient (your JQ), a lot of good things will happen. It may not affect your stress directly. You may indeed have the same number of children, the same mortgage payment, the same days in your work week, the same boss, the same receding hairline, or the same bulging belly. It will, however, affect your *perception* of stress, which ultimately will affect your overall emotional, physical, and spiritual health!

There's a lot of current research on what most folks call "happiness." And maybe their definition of happiness is equivalent to what I'm calling "joy." What's wonderful is that the latest research shows that we do have the power to choose more joy/happiness than perhaps was once thought.

Sonja Lyubomirsky, Ph.D., a psychology professor at the University of California–Riverside, is emerging as one of the gurus of happiness. In her book *The How of Happiness: A Scientific Approach to Getting the Life You Want* (Penguin Press, 2008), she states that research indicates our "happiness" is 50% genetics and 10% circumstances—but a whopping 40% is actually under our control (i.e., what we do and how we think). That's a lot of control, folks! And some of you may even get a head start from your genetics and your circumstances. This means you have no excuse for your lack of joy!

Even before Dr. Lyubomirsky appeared on the scene, Martin Seligman, Ph.D., Director of the University of Pennsylvania Positive Psychology Center (considered to be the "father of positive psychology"), brought the idea of focusing on strengths versus weaknesses, mental health versus mental illness, into public view through paradigm-shifting books like *Authentic Happiness: Using the New Positive Psychology to Realize Your Potential for Lasting Fulfillment* (Simon and Schuster, 2002). So I challenge you to keep reading. You might learn something that will literally change your world (or at least your perception and experience of it).

Take time to savor each chapter. Reread it if necessary, underlining or highlighting the parts that you want to remember or return to for further reflection. Toss the ideas around with a friend or family member to get their feedback about what you have read. Try the Joy Rx Tips as a way of illuminating and reinforcing what you're allowing yourself to consider. Then, go back and look at what you underlined or highlighted. This is for you. This is a gift from my own life and work experience that I want to share, that I simply *must* share. I'm concerned about all of us as human beings in this big, beautiful world. We're missing too much of life and not enJOYing nearly enough of what we are experiencing. Our bodies, minds, and spirits are suffering because of it.

If you decide to embark on this exploration with me, I welcome you. Thank you for taking the time. I hope and pray that you will enJOY the adventure.

In JOY,

Ruth

Section One:

Accept Who You Are

"Strange how little a while a person can be contented."

—*Mark Twain*

Chapter 1: We Are Human—We All Have Basic Needs

"The richest and fullest lives attempt to achieve an inner balance between three realms: work, love and play."

—Erik Erikson

We all need to feel safe. One of the things that often comes up in counseling is the need for security, which ultimately is about the core need for safety. Psychiatrist Erik Erikson, in his *Eight Stages of Development*, talked about the first developmental task being "trust versus mistrust." Can we trust the world in which we find ourselves? That's a very fundamental, critical question.

Each one of us has our own unique history. Even siblings raised in the "same" environment do not have the same experience. We each bring our own genetic makeup and personality; therefore, we experience the world (no matter how big or small) very differently.

13

Most of us, like it or not (it's usually "not"), grew up in what many folks call "dysfunctional families." What this means to me in simple terms is a conditionally loving family versus an unconditionally loving one. That's very basic, but allows the wide variety of families that exist to slip into the category of dysfunctional—even without physical or sexual abuse or domestic violence. Yes, absolutely, outwardly abusive families are well-qualified to be called dysfunctional! Moreover, those families whose abuse or neglect may be more emotional in nature still qualify by virtue of their teaching us, "If you do this or that, or if you don't do this or that, then (maybe) I'll love you and take care of you." That's dysfunction.

Families like that are not "functional" because they are missing the all-important, prime, primal ingredient of safety and a trusting, trustworthy environment. You never know when you'll meet their expectations. It's a constant struggle, trying to second-guess whether you'll please them or fail them, get love or attention (negative or positive). And that's fertile soil for growing anxiety and fear as opposed to safety, security, trust, and self-confidence.

I grew up in a dysfunctional family (surprise!). One of my favorite things to say is that "we put the 'fun' in dysfunctional." We had a strange (but interesting) family. Each of us four kids had a different experience—of course. One of the basics we seem to share is our love of food! I believe one of the reasons we all love food so passionately (I'm not kidding—passionately!) is because family mealtime was often—not always—a time for laughter. I have many fond memories of someone getting "tickled" at something and giggles turning into roars. Plus, Mother was a great cook, which didn't hurt anything at all; in fact, she even had a degree in home economics.

And, not to get too psychoanalytical, but consuming food is a very self-satisfying, self-centered act as well. If there were tensions in the room, we could focus on what was going into our mouths and stomachs, savoring each morsel, while chaos reigned in the outside world. Our physical needs were basically met; our emotional needs were inconsistently met. And food became a very symbolic way in which we all were able to meet our own needs.

You are who you are, where you are, when you are, being the being you simply are. And you deserve to feel good about it! You deserve to feel loved and accepted for who you are—just because. We are human beings, not human "doings." And we all have the right to occupy space

15

on this lovely planet of ours—just because.

Now, I'm saying that's the raw material. It doesn't mean you have to be totally satisfied with where you are, without looking to make yourself and your life move in the direction of your highest self, your authentic self, your self-actualized self. Nevertheless, the place from which that comes is, at its core, acceptance.

If you happen to be one of the majority of folks who come from a dysfunctional family, you may not automatically know what you need. At gut level, you most certainly know a lot of things you don't want or don't like. Sometimes, you find that out in very self-defeating, self-destructive ways. You may try this or that, including relationships, before you realize what you're being attracted to is precisely what you grew up with—and precisely what you *didn't* like/want/need.

Hopefully, you've found a person or two whom you have discovered you can trust, which also helps in developing a sense of trust in the larger world. Perhaps they can be the ones to help you discover some of the things that are healthy, healing, supportive, and nurturing for you. Sometimes someone outside your own very personal existence can be well suited to give you the feedback you need.

If you didn't get the unconditionally loving parenting we all need, then learning to "parent" yourself can help your developing self learn and grow.

And often it's helpful to find someone outside your inner circle, like a clergy person, a psychotherapist, a mentor, a life coach—someone not directly involved in your day-to-day life—to shed some light on your path for you.

Joy Rx Tip for Chapter 1

When you're feeling particularly overwhelmed by your own perceived neediness, grab a pen and paper (or a laptop or handheld device if that's your preference), and find a nice quiet spot. Write down the first *need* that comes to mind. If that is what feels overwhelming at the moment, that specific need is probably not being met. What is the underlying feeling? See if you're able to identify that as well. Are you tempted to cover up that feeling with something that may create even more unmet needs later on?

A somewhat silly (or not) example may be: "I need chocolate and I've already had my quota of calories for the day!" What is the underlying feeling? Loneliness? Boredom? Looking at the underlying feeling may allow you to seek a different way to address the need. Would chocolate fulfill the need for companionship, for example? Learning to write down what's circling around in your mind can be very helpful at times. Give it a try!

Chapter 2: We Are All Unique—One of a Kind

"You don't need anybody to tell you who you are or what you are. You are what you are!"

—*John Lennon*

None of us is perfect, correct? Actually, that's probably up for discussion! My belief is that our Creator doesn't make junk. Yes, there are people whose plight in life I don't personally understand and folks who have a very different way of looking at life than I do. I don't, however, believe I was put here on Earth to decide who is right and who is wrong, or whose life has purpose and whose doesn't. I believe I am here to make the most of my unique characteristics, traits, talents, and abilities.

We all have warts and blemishes. Our Creator made us that way. That's all a part of the outside covering. I believe our "innards"—our souls or spirits—are perfect creations. And who is to say that warts or blemishes are imperfections anyway? Few of us are anywhere close to the limited/limiting images of beauty portrayed in the media. Nor will we ever be!

A friend of mine came up with a word when we were in our wild and crazy 20s—"weirdnesses." I like it! Personally, I'm proud to be "weird." Our daughter (now in *her* wild and crazy 20s) had periods of not appreciating her mother's weirdnesses. One of my quirks is that I'm fairly conscientious about saving and recycling (I'm glad that's finally becoming a respectable trait!). I always stick leftover napkins from a fast food meal into my purse. In fact, I've also been known to grab a plastic fork or spoon, wipe it off, and stick it into my purse for reuse later. And only recently has our daughter begun to see the benefits of another habit I've had since childhood—namely, shopping for used clothing. Before she faced the challenges of budgeting, it was embarrassing for Mom to proudly claim, "I only paid $1.50 for this!"

Fortunately, our daughter is now able to smile (and sometimes laugh) about my weirdnesses. In fact, she gave me a plaque that says, "I live in my own little world, but at least they know me here!" It's hanging on our bedroom wall. I'm quite proud of being weird, and I have a lot of so-called "weird" friends. A compliment (truly!) that our daughter recently paid to a couple of my friends was, "They're the least weird of your weird friends!" And yes, ladies and gentlemen, they too were proud of that esteemed honor!

I've already shared a little about my family. We siblings (there are four) look quite different from one another. Our exteriors are quite unique, and the "embellishments" (i.e., clothing styles, etc.) are definitely "one of a kind" as well. One of our parents was pretty well qualified as a nonconformist, which may have somehow genetically pre-programmed our rather excessive individuality. We've each found our own way in the world—along different pathways—but we do share some similarities.

If you weren't blessed with an unconditionally loving, positively reinforcing family, you may not have learned much about how to give or receive positive attention. Along with that, you may not yet recognize your own potential. You may not even be able to identify your own strengths—but you have them. They may not match anyone else's in your circle of friends or colleagues; however, your strengths do have value. Discovering them is a big part of the journey.

Finding ways to use them in creating a life path for yourself is another huge piece. As you discover and use your strengths, gifts, and talents, you'll realize that you—as unique and wonderful and one-of-a-kind as you are—can become the amazing person you were meant to be.

Joy Rx Tip for Chapter 2

Try listing your strengths. Use your own creativity, if that's a strength, or consult a friend to get someone else's view on your strengths. Another option would be to go to Dr. Martin Seligman's website, www.authentic happiness.org, and take the survey of character strengths.

Martin Seligman and Christopher Peterson together authored the VIA Classification of Character Strengths (2003), exploring the twenty-four strengths that define what's best about people—universally. More information about the VIA classifications can be found at www.viacharacter.org.

The twenty-four strengths are grouped in six categories: wisdom and knowledge, courage, love, justice, temperance, and transcendence.

What are the themes of your strengths? The delight of discovering your strengths is in your own uniqueness. Share your discoveries with others if you choose. Are there themes among your friends? Colleagues? Family?

Chapter 3: Part of Accepting Oneself Is Accepting One's History

"History is the version of past events that people have decided to agree upon."

—Napoleon Bonaparte

By now you know that a large portion of my work life has been as a psychotherapist and clinical social worker, working with people with life challenges (personal, interpersonal, family, etc.). So, the folks I see usually have difficult family histories. Often, their stories have lots of pain in them— lots of regret, sadness, anger, abuse, or neglect. A large part of the challenge lies in what to do with the past. Part of accepting ourselves is accepting who we are in the context of our own family of origin and history.

When your history has been particularly toxic, it's often so deeply ingrained in your body, mind, and spirit that you may feel like you need a symbolic exorcism or mommy- or daddy-ectomy (much like a tonsillectomy!). And, of course, if you married your mother or father (a discovery that often takes years to uncover), and have since divorced (or not!), then you may need a husband- or wife-ectomy as well!

Negative, destructive histories and memories don't feel good. Plus, they interfere with your day-to-day functioning. Often, folks are reluctant to forgive, imagining that somehow forgiveness will release the perpetrator(s) from their evil-doing. Instead, forgiveness is a releasing of the tentacles of pain that entangle you!

Even those toxic individuals in your past may be teachers. Yes, they may teach you what you don't need or want, but they are nevertheless teachers. Thank them, bless them, and let them go on their way. Yes, I do realize that those individuals who have been toxic to you may still be a part of your life! And yes, I realize that makes things difficult. Hopefully, however, you're realizing that you need to have at least a couple of positive, healthy, supportive individuals in your life who hold you up, give you helpful feedback, and stand behind you or beside you on your journey. Those folks are often outside the biological family.

All your experiences create the person you are. They all are part of your makeup. You get to choose if their contribution to your life will be positive or negative. And, if you so choose, the lessons you take from your life experiences will decorate your own internal garden. Sometimes even the stinky stuff is necessary to enrich the soil!

In my family we did have a lot of "stinky stuff" growing up; however, one gift I have—for whatever reason—is that I learned long ago to hang on to the good stuff. There were lots of arguments, lots of screaming matches (it was a very loud household a lot of the time), sometimes even physical encounters. I've been able to erase a lot of those from my memory banks (thank you very much!). But there are many good things I've managed to hang on to, like a day of lovely kite-flying in a field outside one of the small towns where we lived for a year or two. We made box kites—and all six of us had a day outside, watching our kites disappear into the heavens, being reminded of them by the constant tug on the string. It really felt like a little piece of heaven—one glorious day!

I've truly learned to focus on the good stuff that was a part of my childhood. Genetically, we were blessed with "pre-wiring" for musical gifts, for mathematical acuity, decent brain power, and communication skills (I have ancestors who were storytellers, writers, and teachers). Okay, so a few obsessive-compulsive traits got thrown into the mix as well. And blue eyes. And to my daughter's chagrin— big hips! Even in the physiological category, it's best to make the best of what you have to work with.

Joy Rx Tip for Chapter 3

Since accepting your past may include both positives and negatives, making peace with your past is sometimes more difficult than just declaring, "It's done, it's over, I'm good with it!"

One helpful tool is letter-writing. Writing a letter to someone who hurt you in the past can be very healing. The act of writing down one's thoughts can potentially reveal hidden blessings in a relationship previously perceived as purely negative. The person may still be living; if so, you may choose not to send the letter (it is, of course, up to you!).

It's at least equally helpful to write a letter to someone to whom you wish to express gratitude. Part of accepting our past is often done with gratitude. These types of letters can be delivered—and are usually treasured by the recipient. Even if the person or persons have passed on, letter-writing can still be very helpful. Delivered or not delivered, the writing itself can be very healing.

Section Two:
Be Aware, Awake, and
Present for Life

"A rock pile ceases to be a rock pile the moment a single man contemplates it, bearing within him the image of a cathedral."
—*Antoine de Saint-Exupery*

Chapter 4: Pay Attention—Tune In to What's Right in Front of You

"It's not what you look at that matters, it's what you see."

—Henry David Thoreau

One of the hazards of being the kind of woman who enjoys lots of things is that whatever gets my interest keeps my interest—until the next thing comes along. This frustrates the heck out of my husband, for one. Our daughter diagnosed me with something she lovingly called "NDD," or "Nature Deficit Disorder" (versus the more familiar ADD, Attention Deficit Disorder). Not that I have a nature deficit. In fact, it's just the opposite: I can be driving along, fully involved in a conversation, and in a split second, a cloud formation or an interesting tree or a hawk soaring through the trees and clouds will catch my attention, and there I go. Perhaps "Nature Distraction Disorder" would be more appropriate!

It's a gift, and at times a curse. The gift part of it is that I do—for the most part—live moment to moment. Yes, I do plan, and I do lead a relatively orderly life (again, others may have a different viewpoint when observing my sometimes erratic behavior). However, when someone or something is before me, I usually am able to give him, her, or it my full attention.

There are so many gifts in nature. Even the tiniest can be delightful and fascinating, if you're simply observant. To me, even architecture—yes, human-made creations of wood, stone, and metal—can be very appealing to the eye and to the soul. Sometimes I enjoy taking pictures as I observe the beauty all around me. And people-watching is a blast as well. Faces. All ages. All shapes and sizes. All have their own stories to portray.

I will always treasure a memory of our daughter when she was only two or three years old. She was outside in a little inflatable pool, having a blast in her own little world. I noticed her playing with an odd thing she was holding in her fingers. When I realized it was a slug, instead of squealing and frightening her needlessly, I encouraged her to "be nice" to the little critter. So, she proceeded to pet the chubby, slimy creature. Then, before I could stop her, she brought it to her lips and planted a loving smooch on its back. "Yuck!" is what I thought, but she was simply heeding my suggestion. Yes, this was one of God's creatures, and we need to be nice to all of God's creatures, no matter how small (or slimy)!

One of my concerns about the rapidly changing world in which we live is the impact of technology. All the gadgets we now try to manage have made being "present" rather confusing at times. It may seem as if we're very present when we make instant phone connections with others; however, instead of allowing us to be fully present, this seems to make us less present. Our focus is jarred out of the "now" straight into something else, almost without our consent. Multi-tasking is not necessarily something to brag about, in my estimation. It's a built-in symbol of only dealing with things on the surface, rarely allowing much depth of attention. It's as if we're all just stones skipping along the surface of a pond—never able to be anywhere but where the stone touches the water, never able to explore the depths.

Be aware of where you are, who you are, and what's in your environment. Notice. Pay attention. It's a gift, a present—the present. If you're somewhere else, you may miss out on something amazing!

Joy Rx Tip for Chapter 4

If you are caught up in the distractions of technology (it's hard not to be these days, isn't it?), why not take a conscious "tech break" instead of a smoke break (most of us are non-smokers, by now, aren't we?). Turn off the phone, the computer, the TV. Focus on something in nature—in person, in a photograph or work of art, or in your imagination or memory. It could be a leaf, the bark of a friendly old (or young) tree, or an insect walking on the window sill. You could even focus your attention on something like your pet's fur or a person's eyes or hands—or even your own fingers or toes.

You could even get adventurous and give yourself a hand or foot massage. A gift to yourself. A present. The present. EnJOY!

Chapter 5: Be Open to New Experiences

"Imagination will often carry us to worlds that never were. But without it we go nowhere."

—Carl Sagan

It's easy to get into a rut. Routine and rut almost sound the same. Routines can be good, and yet ruts are seen as bad. I try to establish routines for things that I know are healthy for me—like exercise, taking my supplements, sleeping. A rut might be always doing the same thing at the same time, every day.

Life in my family of origin was anything but boring! There were rituals and ruts, for sure, but there were also surprises. We moved a lot, so we were forced into new experiences almost every year, like it or not. My father was a teacher and administrator. Sadly, he wasn't a people person. He was at heart an introvert. His public persona was just that—a persona. He had to act in order to be in public. It was not natural at all. He chose teaching because of his love of music. He wanted to teach music; I never knew why he ended up in administration. He didn't qualify for big school districts. Instead, he had to settle for teeny, tiny little districts. One community we lived in had three students in its graduating class. I often wondered if any of them went on to college. I guess you could say, "I graduated third in my class," leaving out the fact that you also finished last.

Since my father was not a people person, he had a difficult time keeping a job, since the kind of job he continued to go after required people skills. He eventually got the message and left the teaching profession, but not until he had given it every effort. Some call that persistence. I call it stubbornness, with a little bit of obsessive-compulsiveness thrown in.

Each new community brought with it new sights, new people, new classmates, and a new church. So each year, we had to start all over, settling into a new home. One good thing was that we kept boxes handy so we could pack up easily. Another good thing was never having to do any spring cleaning; we weren't in one place long enough for anything to get too dirty.

I suppose that as children, we had no choice about having all these new experiences. And yet, I believe that regularly having to restart in a new community helped me appreciate new experiences more than most folks.

Research is showing that it's stimulating to the brain (and may even create new neural pathways) to change things up every now and then. Try something new like a puzzle or a game. Even better, try something challenging! If you've been doing the same crossword puzzles from the same newspaper for years, try one from a different newspaper. Take a different route to work—you might get lost, but think of the fun you'll have trying to find your way. Better yet, try a different route home—that way the boss won't fuss when you're late. You may come home to a husband, wife, or roommate waiting at the door with a look of disdain or concern, welcoming you with open arms (and new neural pathways, too!).

Or you might try something fun like having a "backwards day," saying "good night" when you get up in the morning and "good morning" when you go to bed. This is particularly fun if you have children. If it's a weekend, you could even have the kids put on their clothes backwards, walk backwards, etc. Fun!

Joy Rx Tip for Chapter 5

If you tend to live by the calendar, clock, or a constant to-do list, take a break from it every now and then. Declare a "timeless" zone for an afternoon or—be daring—even a whole day! See how it feels. Eat when you are actually hungry instead of when the clock hits a certain number. Get up when you naturally awaken instead of waiting for the alarm (or the fifth punch of the snooze button). It can be a well-deserved break from routine.

If you live with family, take turns introducing something new to each other. (Even if it's just you and your pet hamster, you can still try new things.) No matter what age you (or they) are, designate one day or afternoon a week as a "let's try something different" day. Try out that amazing imagination of yours! You may even learn something from those chronologically less endowed than you. And, as long as it's safe and affordable, it'll probably be fun!

Chapter 6: Be Conscious and Intentional About Your Life Path

"It's useless to hold a person to anything he says while he's in love, drunk, or running for office."

—*Shirley MacLaine*

Feeling good about who you are comes from feeling good about what you're choosing in your life, for your life. A large part of being aware and awake and present for life is intentionality. Living a conscious life, being aware of the choices you're making, and consciously, conscientiously choosing is central to feeling good about yourself.

Too many people in this world follow a life path determined by others. The measuring stick they hold themselves and their choices up to is often more related to material/external signs of success than internal/eternal kinds of markers. Our American culture emphasizes monetary wealth and possessions more than personal satisfaction. The overriding cultural goal is to have more stuff, bigger stuff. To be content with what you have is simply not acceptable; therefore, if and when you accept the cultural norms, it's way too easy to be unhappy with yourself or your life.

In my family, we didn't experience any real pressure from our parents to pursue any particular career. We came from a long line of teachers and farmers, so anything that would get us into (and successfully out of) college seemed to be acceptable. The older two siblings made it through college; the younger two didn't. The standards seemed to change to accommodate the children's different dreams and aspirations, which was okay. Finding something we each wanted to do as a career path was important—as long as it kept us from coming back home and landing on our parents' doorstep.

Not everyone in the world is able to choose the perfect career or the perfect family (and once again, who gets to decide what "perfection" is?). Being aware of and conscious about the choices that you make tremendously increases your sense of being joyful in life. Feeling that there are no choices, or that you were somehow robbed of choice, is a very joy-stealing kind of experience.

Being very intentional about your path—not only which path you take but also who travels the path with you—is very joy-producing.

There's a lot of talk these days about setting one's intention. I believe in writing things down. Of course, I enjoy writing, so that comes quite naturally to me; however, I often suggest it to clients as well. Allowing thoughts and ideas to take form enough to make it onto a piece of paper or into a document on your computer changes something. The thought becomes more real. It begins to have form, to take shape. Once it's written down or spoken, it's even more available to be molded into what you want it to be.

Voicing your intentions doesn't lock them into permanent form. All of life is a process. One moment flows into the next. You can speak or write your intentions about anything—your family, your career, your contribution to the betterment of humanity, even your desire to drop the ten pounds you've been battling for a decade or more. It's one more way of being conscious and present.

Identifying your intentions and moving forward is all about living "on purpose." Purposeful living gives life meaning. Living a meaningful life brings joy.

Joy Rx Tip for Chapter 6

Try writing your own mission statement. It can be as vague or specific as you like.

How do you see yourself (remember those strengths you identified)? What do you value in life? How do you envision your life moving forward in the next few years? If this inspires you, use it as a tool to set goals for yourself, both long- and short-term. If everything you've written down has already been accomplished, then it's time to set some new goals. Do these goals fit within your overall mission statement?

Section Three:
Experience Life Fully

"When you look upon another human being and feel great love toward them, or when you contemplate beauty in nature and something within you responds deeply to it, close your eyes for a moment and feel the essence of that love or that beauty within you, inseparable from who you are, your true nature. The outer form is a temporary reflection of what you are within, in your essence. That is why love and beauty can never leave you, although all outer forms will."

—*Eckhart Tolle,* Stillness Speaks *(New World Library, 2003)*

Chapter 7: Use All Your Physical Senses

"Everybody needs beauty as well as bread, places to play in and pray in, where nature may heal and give strength to body and soul."

—*John Muir*

We are multi-sensory beings. We see, we hear, we smell, we touch, we taste. Often we become numb to some of the most sensory-expanding experiences possible. Even eating (especially over-eating) can end up being just a mind/body numbing experience. The sense of being overly full is not a pleasant one. Recall of the nuances of a meal just completed is often lost due to a rushed mealtime or an on-the-run-mealtime (standing, driving, etc.).

I fondly recall sharing a meal with a woman from French Quebec. It almost sounds like a caricature to describe her culinary delight. In her own delightful way, she savored each morsel, taking her time, truly tasting each of the assorted flavors, being with the food, receiving both nourishment and joy.

Over-indulging in other experiences of the senses can be numbing as well. Once again, a lot of something isn't necessarily better than a little. Sipping a glass of wine will probably be more enjoyable than guzzling a whole bottle. The list of potential addictive behaviors has grown in the last few years. Now, in addition to "traditional" addictions like food, alcohol, sex, and gambling, there are also new addictions added to the list of challenges. And the list is growing rapidly, barely keeping up with expanding technology. There are even twelve-step programs developing to address Internet addiction, Internet pornography addiction, shopping addiction, etc.

Getting as much as you can of something or someone is seldom deeply satisfying. One theory about addictions is that, once the "quick access" to a "high" is discovered—particularly if it's discovered before the deeper, more lasting kinds of "highs" are discovered—addiction takes root. Another piece of this is our inability to savor life—whether the piece of life in front of you is a morsel of food or a loving partner. When you fail to learn to savor the life in front of you, "quick fixes" bring an instant rush of excitement—perhaps an adequate substitute, at least for the moment. Those moments, however, are not sustainable. Learning to savor life naturally is.

Parents take note. Allowing your children to discover the delight of their senses early on—from squishing mud between their toes to catching snowflakes on their tongue—is good insurance (although not guaranteed, I'll add) against later "need" for substitute sensations.

Aromas are powerful. One story I love to tell is about a drive I took with our daughter one early spring evening. Being with her was already a plus, a positive warm fuzzy feeling. We were headed to pick up a pasta dish a friend had prepared as a surprise for my husband (his favorite, of course). We were riding in my relatively new car that I actually got to pick out (first time ever!), so even the drive was enjoyable. The temperature of the air was absolutely perfect—the windows were rolled down, the sunroof open. My ears were happy, too, since we had George Benson playing some rhythmic jazz tunes on the stereo. I was already feeling what I like to call a natural "high." All my senses were engaged when something amazing deepened the experience even more: we passed some honeysuckle bushes along the road. As their delicious scent sailed through the open windows, I felt pure sensual joy. My, oh my. That truly was a natural high. Ahh. Whoa!

Our sweet daughter learned from her "weird" mama to enjoy sunsets and rainbows and cloud formations. And ice cream and kittens. Sensual pleasures are gifts to be savored at any age.

Joy Rx Tip for Chapter 7

Challenge yourself to truly experience something you ordinarily take for granted. It could be in the category of taste, aroma, or texture, or even the face (or toes!) of a loved one. Try letting something you ordinarily chew dissolve in your mouth. Hold a piece of velvet against your skin with your eyes closed. Let your shower be a waterfall in a rainforest, and treasure each little droplet that touches your skin. Savor the experience like never before.

If you're at a loss for something to re-experience, why not try our first experiment in high school chemistry. During that class, we were asked to observe and describe—including every detail imaginable—a burning flame on a candle. Only this time, you'll be doing it for you—not for a grade in chemistry. You could try a candle (scented or not), or a campfire or fireplace. Just be careful—once you allow yourself to savor even a flame, it truly can be deliciously hypnotic and surprisingly satisfying.

If you have children in your world, listen to their suggestions. Encourage them to savor things they experience (yes, this may even include touching their food or contact with things you may consider less than sterile), and allow them to invite you into their own wonderful world of imagination. What a delight!

Chapter 8: Connect to Life (Big L) Internally

"This is my simple religion. There is no need for temples; no need for complicated philosophy. Our own brain, our own heart is our temple; the philosophy is kindness."

—*Dalai Lama*

Experiencing life through your senses is of course very physical. Connecting to Life ("big L" as I call it) is on a different plane—more internal than external or physical. We all have our own particular way to do that.

I have a friend who created a labyrinth with stones in her backyard. She follows its pathway in a walking meditation. There is also sitting meditation, where you allow yourself to be still and listen.

We live in such a busy world that quiet may not come as naturally as it once did. There is usually a television or radio or stereo blasting when we're at home. Even at work, there may be noise or sounds coming from computers or simply chatter of some kind. So, quiet is also something that requires intention.

And it's even more challenging to be quiet on the inside.

When our outside world is busy and noisy, our inside world is busy and noisy as well. If and when we allow ourselves to stop the busy-ness, stop the noise, it's amazing what will sift through. The more moments we take to consciously allow stillness, the closer we are to plugging into the big L, Life—to our own core, our own deep connection to the Creative Source, God within. I believe we can plug into something so much bigger, so much greater, so much deeper and pervasive than what we usually experience. Once plugged in, what I like to refer to as experiences of synchronicity (or the "cosmic coincidences" of life) seem to accelerate. The sense of oneness is heightened. And to me, the sense of connectedness is one of joy, the kind you can feel all the way to your toes. Yum.

Not everyone needs to get into a full lotus position to meditate. You may have a favorite chair in your house, a favorite rock by the side of a stream, a favorite tree. You could even be bed bound and have a favorite place in your imagination (real or of your own creation) to go to where you can access that inner calm.

When I have a client who seems to be very caught up in the busy-ness of life (as is the case with most of us!), I frequently offer suggestions about adding meditation to their repertoire. Focusing on your breath—being aware and conscious of the rhythmic flow of the air that fills your lungs, literally fueling life—can be hypnotizing in itself. As you are drawn into the rhythm, the beauty of stillness can take over your consciousness. Focusing on your breath is a lovely way to begin to discover the joy of meditation.

Of course, if you're like most folks, distractions quickly interfere, leaving you frustrated to the point of giving up. For this reason, I often suggest using something to guide you in the beginning, until you get comfortable with the quiet. Even having some background noise can help. In my office, I have a gentle stream flowing invisibly in the background.

To deal with internal distractions, it often helps to have a word or mantra of your choosing. Some disciplines suggest having a "sacred word" to come back to when you get distracted. It is suggested that you choose a word that has no connection to anything in your world that would pull you away from the desired serenity. I use the word "home." For me, it has the "ohm" sound of the universal syllable/sound. And, unlike many for whom "home" might bring images of particular people, places, or even conflict, for me "home" brings an all-encompassing sense of being at home in the world.

The distractions inevitably come; however, over time, as you allow your word to push out any invasive thoughts or images, you will inevitably go deeper. And deeper. As you begin practicing meditation, you will find yourself even more connected to your inner core, the deepest parts of yourself which are ultimately connected to the Source of All, our Creator.

Wherever your place, take yourself there as often as you can and will. Meditation will feed your spirit.

Joy Rx Tip for Chapter 8

Try finding or creating your own meditation time. Just five minutes at a time can help. Taking even one minute to pause in your busy day can be a delightful, energizing, deepening gift to yourself. It can be as simple as closing your eyes where you sit—in a car, at your desk, in bed (morning or evening or both)—and focusing on your chosen word or on your breath moving in and out. Breathe in goodness and renewal, breathe out any stress or unwanted feelings or thoughts. Committing to a couple of pauses in your day may create a desire for more. And, as you begin to receive the benefits, you'll hopefully want to increase the space and time allotted for these positive pauses.

Chapter 9: Feel Your Feelings—Even the Difficult Ones

"The art of living is more like wrestling than dancing."

—*Marcus Aurelius*

One destructive thing that I believe contributed to my own father's death by cancer was his inability to express any feeling other than anger. At his funeral, his mother (in her 90s at the time) told us through tears about how he had learned as an infant that it did no good to cry. Grandmother was not able to comfort him when he needed her. Her demanding husband insisted that she leave her precious firstborn baby alone while she cared for the workers on the farm. Though I'll admit this sounds way too simplistic, as an adult he did not show positive emotion. Instead he would explode into negative emotions. Sad.

Feelings are real. One of the coolest things about being human is the range of emotion we are able to experience.

Working in psychotherapy, I often found myself sending folks home with pages of faces labeled with feeling words, or simply dozens of names of feelings. We often don't give children the words to express the vast array of feelings at our disposal. If we only give kids the words *mad*, *glad*, and *sad*, one third of our feelings are "mad." I don't believe that large a portion are truly angry feelings. And if anger makes up a large portion of your own emotional repertoire, it may be time to look a little deeper. Trust me, if you take the time to look you'll find a lot below the surface.

I've worked with children and families extensively in my practice of psychotherapy. Even grown-ups tend to see and express anger as a huge part of their emotional repertoire! There is so much more. Even to discover the nuances of disappointment and frustration, for example, versus "simple" anger, can expand verbal and expressive feelings.

Life is hard! Avoiding negative feelings is impossible. Pushing feelings aside, hoping to avoid having to face them often causes them to come out "sideways" later on. I saw this occur a lot in working with children who had experienced trauma of one kind or another. Learning that there are safe and healthy ways to express emotions is a valuable tool we can give our children. Of course, one of the most powerful ways we can teach them is by modeling healthy ways of feeling and expressing emotions ourselves.

Allowing yourself to feel the full range of emotions brings with it the contrast and the depth of human emotion. Just as it aches in an uncomfortable way to experience pain and despair, so it "aches" in a good way to feel the intensity of joy.

I believe it actually requires energy to avoid hurt feelings, anger, and other negative emotions. One visualization I often suggest is a "protective suit" to be put on in the morning when crawling out of bed. For folks who are sensitive to the energy of others, a protective suit of one kind or another (some like the "armor" concept) is helpful in getting through your day, particularly if you're exposed to a lot of negativity.

Wearing a protective garment allows you to choose what you let in and what you don't. It's nice! Consequently, you don't have to be attacked by other people's garbage or prickly feelings. Children have great imaginations as well.

They can often understand this creative form of self-protection more easily than grown-ups. It can be a helpful tool if there are other children throwing potentially hurtful jabs in their direction!

Joy Rx Tip for Chapter 9

Try on your own protective suit. Zip it up before you get out of bed in the morning. You may even choose to add a helmet as an extra safety feature. Your suit may be as thick or impenetrable as you feel is needed. Or, if you prefer a different concept, you might like to imagine a bubble or an egg of sorts—with a shell or skin to keep you safe inside. Children and adults can utilize this daily, or just at special times when extra comfort or safety is desired.

Feel free to fill it with whatever concept of energy or softness you like. It can shine or twinkle, feel soft and cozy or light and airy. It's strictly for you, so make it according to your own chosen design.

Chapter 10: Energy Can Be Healing—Allow It to Be

"The energy of the mind is the essence of life."

—*Aristotle*

The more we explore the levels and layers of life, the more microscopically we look at ourselves and the air and space around us, the more we realize we are all simply energy of one kind or another. We're all little atoms and molecules bouncing around in the air. What we imagine is solid really isn't.

So what is inside us and outside us is just that—energy.

If we're really learning to tune into Life in a healthier way, we're going to become more aware of our own "energy" as well as that of others. Some of us may have already been tuning in for a while. If so, what another's energy feels like may be uncomfortable—even thick or sticky! It's almost as if we're going beyond the five senses. That's all right. Our world is multi-dimensional; why can't we be multi-sensory?

That protective suit I just mentioned can come in quite handy as you become more sensitive to others' energy. And, speaking of energy, as you become more aware of energetic connections to others, allow yourself to be open to the positive energy that comes from all of creation, and even from the Creator.

When I was a child, I remember seeing pictures in Sunday school of Jesus and his mother, Mary, with halos over their heads. It was as if they had this glowing force above their heads. I like to imagine divine energy as light. Sometimes it seems like white light, other times it may seem golden. Whatever the color or energy at the time, I also can imagine it coming into me—"zapping" me with a loving, nurturing kind of warmth. And I let it come into me from my own crown, the top of my head. Somehow this makes sense. Not that I have delusions of grandeur, thinking I'm eligible for my own halo; however, it just feels right to allow that rejuvenating force to come in through my crown.

I've had some amazing experiences with a healing practice called "Healing Touch Therapy." In the training, the instructors speak of the chakras and meridians, both ancient concepts used in healing practices. The crown is the seventh chakra, the one that represents our connection to the Source, the Creator, God. Makes sense to me!

Overall, increasing sensitivity to the energy all around you and within you can expand, deepen, and enrich your experience of joy.

Joy Rx Tip for Chapter 10

Remember the bubble or protective suit we spoke of in chapter 9? Add the concept of energy, and you can fill your bubble or protective suit with the most divine, energizing fuel imaginable! When you need refueling, envision your crown opening up. If it helps (and this works well with children), picture the divine equivalent of a gas pump. Imagine God pumping energy directly into you as brilliant white or gold light, filling every part of your body, warming you, and making you tingle with joy—the deep-down, luscious variety.

Chapter 11: Soak Up the "Highs"

"Life loves the liver of it."

—*Maya Angelou*

I mentioned my experience of a natural high while driving with our daughter. One "trick" is learning to take these highs and make them a part of you.

I often help clients identify their "happy place" in an effort to improve their ability to relax. We may practice going there in the office (eyes closed, of course). I also suggest they take the image of their "happy place" with them when they go home, asking them to essentially memorize their vision, employing all their senses as much as possible to literally imprint it in their mind, heart, and soul. Discovering some kind of inner vision/visualization that brings a smile to one's insides and outsides is often a delightful surprise. Learning to hold on to something so good (whether it's real or imagined!) is great practice. Being able to feel that good (i.e., safe, comfortable, peaceful, content, filled with deep joy) using just your own imagination—whether you retrieve the imagery from an actual memory or create it from some other picture in your mind—is an amazing example of how truly powerful our minds are.

For me, music can trigger happy places, happy memories. I can literally feel "high" at almost a moment's notice by putting on a favorite piece of music. Depending on the type of "high" I'm seeking, I might choose a driving, loud, intense song or a quiet, melodic symphonic piece. Again, the trick to building up your inner resources of joy is learning to incorporate these joy-making moments into your everyday life. Storing up all the good stuff builds resources for when life hits you with something hard.

Optimism is a gift with which I was blessed. I truly think I was "wired" to look on the bright side. I can usually find something to smile about. I have stories galore about real-life instances of turning strange and often icky experiences into positive ones. Having stored-up joy certainly helps!

I have had several vehicles that had assorted idiosyncrasies (not surprising!). One had a congenital defect in addition to being rather magnetic. I was blessed to discover its magnetism within the first brief month of ownership. I was traveling with a dear friend when another driver decided to cross a few lanes of traffic to make a left turn. My poor car was unfortunately in the way. The car already had a dent in the left fender (scheduled to be fixed by the former owner upon our return). So, with my traditional cheery, optimistic attitude, upon discovering a newly dented fender, I exclaimed, "Well, at least now they match!" My fellow vacationer couldn't help but laugh. It is often a great alternative to tears!

Joy Rx Tip for Chapter 11

Music is a great tool. Experiment with it a little. Try different recordings (live music is great, too, if you're lucky enough to know or be a musician!). See what styles of music move you. Perhaps there's one particular recording that sends you soaring or straight into tears. It may be the words or the rhythm or the instrumentation. Whatever the connection, it's a connection to your deeper self. Allow it to bring a more intense experience.

Or, for a more visual experience, the next time you spot a glorious sunset on the horizon, stop your car or your feet (if it's safe, of course!) and soak it in. Most of us don't have the opportunity to see the sun set over water every day. If you do, or if you have a memory of it, enjoy every detail.

For an experiment with touch, be very present when brushing your own hair, a child's or partner's hair, or a pet's fur.

No matter which of your senses you are tuning in to, by whatever means, practice "soaking it up"—what a joy!!

Section Four:
Let Go of the Things You Can't Control

"The more clearly you realize your lack of control, the more powerless you discover yourself to be. The more powerless you discover yourself to be, the more natural it is for you to be surrendered to God. The more surrendered to God you become, the less you struggle against the natural flow of life. The less you struggle against the flow of life, the freer you become. Radical powerlessness is radical freedom, liberating you from the need to control the ocean of life and freeing you to learn how best to navigate it."

—Rabbi Rami Shapiro

Chapter 12: No More Woulda-Shoulda-Coulda's

"Given a sufficient number of people and an adequate amount of time you can create insurmountable opposition to the most inconsequential idea."

—*Source Unknown*

Since I work as a psychotherapist, I encounter a lot of individuals who are dealing with the world from the perspective of depression or anxiety.

Anxiety and depression are close cousins. They both view the world as largely "not okay." One difference may be in the activity of the mind. Anxious people over-think things, worrying about all those details they can't control anyway. Depressed people often feel/believe that life has somehow cheated them. A cloud follows them wherever they go. Neither of these states is a place anyone would consciously choose to be or to go; however, many of us are in such a place.

An overly simplistic way of looking at it is that anxiety lives in the land of "what-ifs" and depression lives in the land of "how awful." In either case, it's a very distressing place to live. My brash, bold suggestion is that on the way to joy, a gift we can give ourselves is to begin to recognize what is within our control and what is not.

We have no power or control over the sun coming up every morning. It still does. Sometimes it's behind the clouds; sometimes it's not. Grass continues to grow. Babies of every species imaginable continue to be born. The stars are there, whether they're visible or invisible to us, concealed by clouds or daylight. And people think, feel, and behave in ways they choose, whether we like it or not, whether they consult us or not.

These "woulda-shoulda-coulda's" I'm referring to often seem to be programmed into us practically from birth. We're pre-programmed to want to somehow control things that are not within our control. Plus, we're programmed to want to please others and meet others' expectations. When we discover all the expectations others have of us, we turn right around and expect all kinds of things from them!

I like the Serenity Prayer because it asks for assistance in being able to recognize what's within our control and what's not. That's no easy task. We need all the help we can get!

The Serenity Prayer, usually attributed to theologian Reinhold Niebuhr and adopted by most twelve-step programs, is as follows:

> God, grant me the serenity
> To accept the things I cannot change;
> The courage to change the things that I can;
> And the wisdom to know the difference.

I have worked with many people who literally make themselves sick fretting over what others think, what others say. They also set themselves up for disappointment over and over by expecting unreasonable things from others; we ultimately have no control over other human beings anyway!

That optimism thing comes in here as well. If we think/believe that ultimately the positive will overcome the negative, that everything will work out all right, and that—bottom line—all is right with the world, we tend to be happier and less anxious. So, part of the journey of healing from depression and anxiety is truly about turning around your thoughts.

Increasing your experience of the positive, joyful, joy-filled aspects of life can't help but reduce symptoms of anxiety and depression.

I imagine that those of you who have experienced anxiety and/or depression for years, decades, or a lifetime may choose to throw this book out the window. "That's way too simplistic!" you may mutter or scream. But I continue to believe that inch by inch, moment by moment, if you allow yourself to notice, savor, treasure, and hold on to little morsels of joy, you will begin to discover the gift you're giving yourself.

Changing your internal thoughts, feelings, and perceptions, and changing your external experiences, can truly be transformative.

Joy Rx Tip for Chapter 12

Write the Serenity Prayer on a piece of paper. Keep it with you in different places—your office, your car, your bathroom mirror. When you find yourself facing a challenge—feeling or believing you should have done something, or someone else should have done something differently, or the outcome could have been different—first, take a deep breath. Then read the prayer. If you're not particularly religious, don't let the "prayer" concept throw you. You're simply asking for assistance in discerning what is within your power to change and what is not.

Look at the specific situation that's troubling you and assess your power and control over the circumstances, the people involved, etc. Do you ultimately have any power or control? Take another deep breath. Admitting your powerlessness is the first step in any twelve-step program. It's a beginning—and it can be extremely eye-opening.

Chapter 13: No More Reruns or Coming Attractions

"Do not dwell in the past, do not dream of the future, concentrate the mind on the present moment."

—*Buddha*

One of my ways of talking about anxiety is to tell folks that they are often stuck in "reruns" or "coming attractions." They experience what I call "over-thinking," in which their minds are rarely in the present moment. Instead, they are loaned out to the past or the future. Talk about wasted energy. But it's a habit that's hard to break. Many live that way for years until they wake up to the realization that they're missing out on what could be the most happy, joy-filled part of their lives—the now.

I've often reflected on my own life, growing up in my fun but dysfunctional family. Genetically, I realize that

I'm pre-wired to be on the anxious side. It manifests in quirky little ways in me: I'm a compulsive recycler. I'm a compulsive overeater (in my own process of recovery right now, thankfully). I can hold tension arising from anxiety in my body without even realizing it—until a headache abruptly brings it to my attention. Others in my family are workaholics, compulsive savers, etc. I don't know that any of us is the type that gets stuck in the past or future, but I haven't had the privilege of getting inside the heads of my siblings. (I can hear them breathe a collective sigh of relief!) But I would imagine there's probably a significant amount of over-thinking going on in there.

If you think about it, being in the past or future, and thereby not in the present, means you are hanging out in a different time zone. Come back! Come back! Just think of what you may be missing.

This illusion of control somehow makes us think we can change the past. When I succeed in calling someone's attention back to the present long enough to ask, "Can you change anything that's happened in the past?" they consistently answer, "No, of course not." And yet, they still find themselves visiting the past, yearning for things to be different.

Intellectually, they can accept that they can't change things. Once that understanding translates into their deeper awareness, they begin getting closer to the now.

Over-thinkers will often try to convince me that, if they concede it is indeed useless to worry and fret about the past, then by all means, it can't hurt to worry and fret about the future, right? I do understand how tempting it is to believe this. And I'm not completely lacking my own worries. Remember, I do have that genetic trait of anxiety coursing through my veins as well.

I do, however, suggest an alternative to creating disastrous scenarios of "what-if." I believe we have an amazing imagination. We can imagine all kinds of possibilities for the future. Most of the folks I see in my practice tend to see the worst possible future. A pessimist might say, "If I expect the worst, then anything different will be a pleasant surprise." I, on the other hand, believe that the best possible outcome is equally as possible as the worst. So, if I choose to use any of my precious energy forecasting the future, I prefer to imagine the best possible outcome. If you believe that setting your intention helps create your reality and experience, then doesn't choosing a positive scenario to focus upon/visualize/intend sound like the best alternative?

Joy Rx Tip for Chapter 13

If you are constantly bombarded by negative thoughts, practice the "cancel-cancel-cancel" technique. When you find yourself saying negative things to yourself, silently say "cancel" (saying it three times somehow seems to make it more effective in stopping those unwanted thoughts). Immediately, flip that thought upside down—saying/thinking the direct opposite. For example, if you say to yourself, "That was a stupid thing to do!" internally say to yourself, "Cancel, cancel, cancel," and tell yourself something like, "You're a smart person. You can make a good choice this time." Or, if you fear danger coming to you on a road trip, cancel that thought and immediately picture yourself traveling safely to your destination and arriving, rested, with a smile on your face! It can happen!

If you find this is a consistent problem, begin writing your thoughts in a notebook. Draw a line down the middle of the page. On one side, write down your negative thoughts. Beside each thought, on the other side, write a positive thought to counter it. Review these; practice them. Reprogram your brain to immediately think positive thoughts in response to the negatives. At minimum, the negatives will hang around less and less in your consciousness. And who knows—at some point, the positives may even start being your first (and only) thoughts!

Chapter 14: Manage Yourself—Be "in Control"—in the Healthiest Way Possible

"Think what a better world it would be if we all, the whole world, had cookies and milk about three o'clock every afternoon and then lay down on our blankets for a nap."

—*Barbara Jordan*

You may be getting the feeling that I believe lots of things are outside our control. I believe that control is basically an illusion. I believe that we simply cannot control other human beings; and, not surprisingly, those of us who continually try to control others keep hitting our heads against a very strong and quite impenetrable brick wall.

I will, however, admit that when our precious children are tiny, dependent infants, we do have ultimate control over their bodies—and literally over whether they survive and thrive in the world. And the gifts we give them (or deprive them of in the cases of abuse or neglect) do have a great amount of influence on their development in life. We provide nourishment for body, mind, and spirit as long as they are in our care.

Nevertheless, with every day and hour that our children manage to grow older (something we also cannot control, no matter how hard we try), we have less control over their minds and spirits. We do have control over their bodies—to an extent which also decreases every day. (Toilet training is an excellent example of how we do not have complete control over their little bodies; that's one thing they clearly must do for themselves on their own schedule, in their own time!) If your children have been in daycare, there may have been daily reports as to when and how much they ate, how often their diapers were changed, how long they napped, etc. You were made aware of what happened during those hours they were apart from you; however, in the meantime you gave up "control" to other trusted adults.

It's easy to live under the illusion that we know our children—how they think and feel and even how they would react and interact—all the time and in any circumstance. Allowing them to grow up is a difficult thing for us, usually because of our love and at times our fear of how they will deal with a world that seems a bit scary.

We had an eye-opening experience when we took our little three-year-old daughter to the fortieth birthday party of a dear friend. We were aware that there would be very few children there, but we still trusted that she would enjoy herself—after all, it was a pool party and she was already beginning to enjoy being in and around the water. She seemed to be having fun.

What was baffling and a true revelation to us was what happened when we were preparing to leave the party. It was in an enclosed back yard, and the people and the place all felt very safe to us, so there were times when she was walking around and meeting other people away from our constant surveillance. As we said our goodbyes, she asked me to follow her to a different part of the yard. She wanted to say goodbye to her new friend. Her new friend was our age. She—at three years of age—had independently met another grown-up (apparently a very sweet young woman). Our daughter did turn out to be quite a little extravert; but that was my first awakening to the fact that she was her own little person with her own thoughts, feelings, interests, and friends. We were not in control, even though we still may have been operating under that illusion!

What we are in control of is our *own* thoughts, feelings, and behavior. We are responsible for ourselves. Yes, we do have the ability to influence others—our thoughts, feelings, and behavior can have an impact on them. And, yes, we can choose to be a positive or a negative influence in the world. Ultimately, however, it is the choice of those other human beings we encounter whether or not to allow us to have influence over them. It's their choice how to respond. It's our choice how to be in their presence.

Because we have control over ourselves, it makes sense that we would want to take good care of ourselves. That seems logical, but it often escapes our awareness. I haven't even tiptoed into the whole area of "blaming." Talk about a joy-taker. When you point your finger angrily at other people or circumstances, literally giving them power over who you are and who you will become, it can seriously interrupt your ability to retain joy. Hurt and resentment tend to form a cloud over who you are and how you function in life.

When working with a client on a particular problem, we often begin by taking a brief look at what they have experienced in their lives, i.e., family of origin issues. The purpose of this is not to assign blame, but to increase understanding. We are all wounded in one way or another. Healing from wounds can come when you realize you have a choice about who you are and who you choose to become. Continuing to live in the pain of woundedness and lack of forgiveness only delays healing. Discovering your strengths and what raw materials you have to work with is of vital importance to recovering from any type of trauma. Beginning to live your best life possible—in spite of what has happened—is a grand tribute to the human spirit.

We have a responsibility to ourselves and to those with whom we come in contact to attempt to be the best we can be—healthy and happy, fulfilled in every way possible or imaginable. Let's keep imagining. And, as we imagine, we can envision positive steps in our everyday lives that will keep us facing forward with a smile on our faces.

This whole moving forward thing—"being the best we can be"—is, of course, easier said than done. I often tend to be a little butterfly—flitting from one thing to another. Yes, living in the present moment is usually a good thing. For practical reasons, however, I myself have had to find my way into some routines.

Facing some health challenges and changes in work schedules, I tried one thing after another to get regular exercise into my schedule. I eventually found what works for me—literally by trial and error. In choosing what is nutritionally wise and healthy, I may have been more conscious and conscientious than the average person—but finding something easy and workable is still a challenge. As a preventative measure I also researched different supplements and found a combination of things that seems to work—again, for me and my lifestyle.

I finally managed to discover routines that I can adhere to, but that aren't stifling. I persisted because I was and remain committed to caring for my physical self. It's a package deal: we are body, mind, and spirit, so caring for body, mind, and spirit is vital to a joyful, fulfilling existence.

Is it easy? Is it automatic? Some of the avenues to joy I've suggested can indeed become so second-nature that they do seem easy and become automatic. But remember, we are all truly one-of-a-kind and, therefore, it may remain "rocket science" to some folks, literally an uphill battle. Nevertheless, I believe and know in my own body, mind, and spirit that it is worth the effort!

Joy Rx Tip for Chapter 14

When you decide to be conscious and conscientious about your body, mind, and spirit, it often helps to have a little bit of discipline attached. That's harder for some of us than for others. Here are some things that have helped me:

Body: I keep a calendar in our bedroom where I write down how much I exercise each day. At times I've even given myself gold stars or stickers to recognize my achievement. In a separate notebook I keep with me, I also write down what I eat (since I have a tendency to overeat). And I'm a card-carrying lifetime member of Weight Watchers, so I very readily acknowledge the benefits of group support as well.

Mind: Reading of all kinds is helpful, and learning something new is wonderful. Puzzles can also help keep the mind stimulated, as can conversation.

Spirit: Setting aside time for prayer and meditation is a gift you can give yourself. Reading spiritual materials can also be enlightening and inspiring. Decide what fits in that category based on your beliefs and your faith.

Section Five:

Share with Others and

Celebrate Our Oneness

"Alone we can do so little; together we can do so much."

—*Helen Keller*

Chapter 15: Share the Joy—It's Contagious

"You can't stay in your corner of the forest, waiting for others to come to you; you have to go to them sometimes."

—*Piglet (A. A. Milne)*

I've mentioned energy. When you have the joy-filled kind of energy, it will radiate from within. If you allow joy to fill you up from the inside out, others can't help but see it, feel it, even hear it in your voice. It will bubble up and pour out without your even trying.

In contrast, if you live in the past or future and are motivated and "fed" only by fear, that will also be felt by others. It's a different kind of energy, the kind that isn't pleasant.

Which of these two types of energy do you like to be around? It probably depends on what you're looking for.

I believe joy-filled folks are electric and sparkle—maybe even glow! Theirs is the kind of energy that multiplies, smile by smile by smile. They give it off and they don't rob you of any of yours.

The others end up almost as energy-drainers. Their energy is such that you may often feel depleted after being around them. Theirs is a needy type of energy that may rob you of yours (if you allow it), while they search for something they believe they've lost or might need. I guess you can discern my preference!

When you—at the core of your being—are joy-filled, you will want to be with others. Admittedly, there are extraverts and introverts in the world. Not all of us like being in large groups. Some are more comfortable with a couple of friends than with twenty. And some individuals may derive more of their joy factor from nature and four-legged beings than from two-legged beings; however, being with others (of any species) seems to help spread the joy.

If you give yourself the gift of increasing the joy factor in your life, once you're filled to the brim you can't help but share it. And others will be thrilled to catch it from you. Hopefully, they'll be able to soak it up as well. As you live your life from this new or renewed perspective, you will inspire others.

"Love is something if you give it away; you end up having more" is a line from a simple but profound song I sang as a young girl ("Magic Penny," by Malvina Reynolds, 1955). And the motivation to not only share but to serve others inevitably comes as a result.

Joy Rx Tip for Chapter 15

Try wearing a smile to work—greeting others with enthusiasm and an optimistic outlook, offering them a gift with no expectations or strings attached. The only expectation for yourself is that you will have a great day. Begin your day, enter your routine (whether you work at home, at an office somewhere, or in a restaurant or warehouse, etc.), and look forward to a joy-filled day, with your eyes and your smile supporting your overall sense of joy and contentment. It will most likely be reinforced by others' responses and reactions; therefore, as it is returned to you, it will feed your own sense about the day being good . . . and on it goes!

Chapter 16: The Good Old Golden Rule

"Do not do unto others as you would that they should do unto you. Their tastes may not be the same."

—George Bernard Shaw

In all the major world religions, there's the equivalent of what we call the Golden Rule—i.e., treat others as you want to be treated. If you're feeling particularly joyful or joy-filled in the company of others, not only will they feel it naturally, but you'll be setting a superb example of how to take your joyful self into the world. Talk about a good marketing tool for joy! Others will want some of that good stuff. Your behavior is now motivated by that inner sense of being deeply connected to Life, that inner smile. The yearning is to give, to love, to share that which cannot be depleted. Once we start building up our supply, we realize the supply is endless and feeds on itself. Joy is therefore discovered and re-created in giving, in the serving of others. Treating others the way you want to be treated becomes just as natural as breathing.

I believe that I am a healer by nature (don't ask me how I know—I just know!), a peacemaker due to my wacky childhood (I was thrown into that role from an early age), and someone who quite naturally laughs at myself and life. In my growing up years, I saw many things I believed I'd do differently, and a few that I thought were worth keeping.

As I have shared before, ours was a loud household, both parents being screamers. Mother also included crying as part of her emotional repertoire. Of course, those emotional responses carried over to the kids. We were frequently the ones being screamed at. It didn't take too many years before my role became that of a peacemaker. At least I tried to get the others to calm down—not that they complied. I just was never a screamer myself. And, when my peacemaking attempts didn't create the changes I wanted, I decided I'd try my hand at studying the intriguing aspects of human beings through psychology, sociology, and social work. It was one of my ways of treating others the way I wish I had been treated (which may be another corollary of the Golden Rule!).

I'm often asked how I am able to keep doing what I do and not take it home with me (or not be negatively influenced by energy-drainers). For one, I have learned and know completely the limitation of my power (a different way of saying "control") over another human being. I only offer what I can, hoping to somehow help them see or feel or think about things differently, in a way that allows them to begin (or continue on) their path to healing and wholeness. If they allow me to enter into a place of possible influence, I accept that honor and make the most of our time together. When our time is complete, however, I let them go, respectful of their own free will and independence. When a client occasionally pops into my consciousness at another time, I offer a prayer for healing and let go (and "let God," as the saying goes).

Joy Rx Tip for Chapter 16

There's a term being used more and more lately: "random acts of kindness." I like the concept. It encourages gestures toward others with no expectation of "payback" (sound familiar?). Unfortunately, we often think of random acts as being outside our home environment.

That's wonderful, and I don't want to discourage it at all, but for my Joy Rx tip for this chapter I'd like to suggest focusing on your own home front. Or, if you live by yourself, consider a member of your extended family or a neighbor. I'm suggesting this because often, unfortunately, our closest family and friends see us at our worst. They're the ones to whom we forget to say please and thank you, or forget to offer help without being asked. I encourage you to try doing something kind for someone close to you—it doesn't have to be anything huge. If you begin to practice treating those closest to you like you want to be treated (i.e., no longer taking the other for granted), it may change the dynamics of the relationship in a very positive way.

Chapter 17: Practice Daily Gratitude

"This is the day that the Lord has made; let us rejoice and be glad in it."

—*Psalm 118:24, ESV*

The greater the joy you have inside, the more at ease you are with life. The more at ease, the less dis-ease. Whether or not this manifests in your physical self, at least there is ease and lack of dis-ease in your spirit, your essence, that part which is most directly connected to the Universal Consciousness, the Creator, the Source, the Force, one's Higher Power, the Infinite, God.

And with ease of spirit and regular connection to the deeper parts of Life, the oneness of all Life will be obvious and pervasive—so much a part of your existence that it becomes second nature. As it becomes second nature, nature itself may no longer come "second" in your priorities! Before I start sounding like a philosophy or theology 101 professor, I'll share that my deep connection to the planet is something about which I truly feel passionately. I care.

I mentioned earlier my "recycle-itis," as I call it. I'll admit that I reach into trash cans if someone "accidentally" forgets to put an aluminum can in the appropriate bin. I usually don't dig too deeply into trash, but I'll admit I've done it on occasion. I try to be conservative with resources—electricity, water, paper goods, etc. Even if we all don't all become OCD about it, if more of us could minimize our use of resources, recycling (or at least not using as much) plastic, paper, etc. whenever possible, our dear planetary home will appreciate the help. You may not "feel" her like I do, but she is a living organism—a pretty large one, admittedly, compared to the tiny little cells of our bodies. And it's mind-blowing and humbling to see our huge planet Earth in relation to solar systems, galaxies, and star systems beyond our own.

Talk about a reason for gratitude and soul-stirring, heartfelt joy! We have been blessed with an amazing physical vehicle to live in while we're hanging out on this magnificent planet! What an incredible, miraculous creation!

And we truly are one. We just need to recognize it and behave accordingly, treating our fellow human beings more compassionately. When the first astronaut saw Earth from a distance, borders were not visible, just land and water, atmosphere and space. People were not visible. Divisions did not exist.

When you begin being conscious and aware of this unbelievable human existence, realizing this is your everyday experience—walking (if so blessed), talking (if so blessed), and breathing—daily gratitude comes easily.

The miraculous things (like walking, talking, and breathing) are definitely reasons for gratitude. I'll even say a silent (or sometimes audible) "thank you" for so-called little things like getting a parking place quickly at the mall, having a cashier be exceptionally courteous, finding a peaceful solution to a problem at work, or having a child pick up their toys without being asked. All are occasions for gratitude.

Approaching life with an attitude of gratitude every day—literally every moment it pops into your awareness—can be transformative. It can become an awareness and acknowledgement of all that's good in life, reinforcing a connection to Life—big L—that's deep and lasting. As you embrace what's good about you and your life, and connect to the good in people, creation, and the Creator, you can't help but respond in gratitude and, ultimately, in service to others. In giving yourself to others, you will inevitably add to what's already right with the world and to your ever-evolving experience of joy. Cool.

Thank you, thank you, thank you!

Joy Rx Tip for Chapter 17

Most of us have by now heard of and/or used the concept of a gratitude journal. Whatever you choose to write in—a 25-cent spiral notebook or a hand-picked one-of-a-kind journal; however you decide to write about your day (drawing pictures, writing paragraphs, phrases, or words); whenever and wherever you choose to write (in the morning at the kitchen table or in the evening at your bedside), the trick is to actually do it. Regardless of how you choose to do it, acknowledging the gifts of the day inevitably increases your JQ. It just does. If it's a new habit you're creating, you might repeat certain gifts of the day. Things like "I'm grateful that I only woke up once during the night," or "I'm glad the kids did their homework without any arguing," or "I was happy my friend called me today" may show up more than once. But as you get used to the practice, you'll begin paying closer attention; consequently, your awareness will sharpen and your gratitude will expand and even explode—in a good way!

Chapter 18: Reap the Benefits

"When I stand before God at the end of my life, I would hope that I would not have a single bit of talent left, and could say, 'I used everything you gave me.'"

—*Erma Bombeck*

A joy-filled you will be healthier, happier, more able to deal with the inevitable stresses of life, more resilient, more accepting, more wise, and more grateful. You will be more enjoyable to be around, a better partner, mate, employee, parent, or family member. Okay, so I believe in what I'm sharing. Truly. Now, put that into a pill and market it!

Sadly, we're killing ourselves with some of our lifestyle choices. We are the first generation in which life expectancy is rumored to be going down. Lifestyle-related illnesses and stress-related illnesses are literally taking us down one by one. It's got to stop, and we're the only ones with the power and control (over ourselves) to do it!

If you're taking the time to read this book, you care. You care about yourself; you care about who you are and how you behave in the world; you care about who you are with others; and you care about how you experience your life. You want to have more joy in your life! You can and will make a difference—in yourself and others. Even though I've never met you, I thank you for caring and wanting to make a difference.

As you commit to making your life more joyful, you are affirming your willingness to let your own light shine brighter in the world. Your light *will* shine. Your radiance will help light up the world. Just imagine lots and lots of light radiating from all the people infused with joy. All those lights will light up the world—what a glow!

And—not so cosmic but practically helpful—increased joy most definitely reduces your experience of stress. It can give a boost to your immune system, which will reduce physical illness. Feeling better in general increases your ability to manage your life—to stay focused and balanced. Not bad for something you don't have to buy at the grocery store or pick up at the pharmacy. You just have to be awake and aware enough to notice it.

Take a dose of it every day—and *don't* call me in the morning. Instead, give someone you love a big smoochie kiss (even if they're furry and four-legged), tell them you love them, and be prepared to enJOY every day in every way imaginable, recognizing we are all truly blessed.

I am grateful!

Author information:

Ruth R. Williams, LCSW, lives in the Nashville, TN, area with her carpenter/musician husband Jeff and cat/dog Charlie (rumored to be a Maine Coon). They have one daughter, Allie (their pride *and* joy), who is a graduate in Communication Studies from the University of Tennessee.

Ruth is available for one-on-one life coaching and for seminars for your business, organization, or faith community. She also has available a CD of some of her original music (*New People for a New World*) and a meditation/relaxation CD (*Meditation of Joy*). For contact information or to order either of these products, please visit her website, www.ruthwilliams.com.

Made in the USA
Middletown, DE
09 November 2022